Come Ride with Me

Horse Poems for Learning and Enjoyment

by

Mary Beth Brace

COME RIDE WITH ME

If you can come ride with me
Through the creek, across the field,
 And on along the beach by the sea
Or shall we go up scenic trails?
Or go along a deserted path?
Don't be alarmed
If we are caught in the rain.
Have a horse's kind of bath!
Adventures wait…
What's around the next bend?
What gifts does nature to us send?
Horse ears prick forward
Alert to movement and sound.
A white tail flash of runaway deer,
Calls from bird song drift to the ear.
Mesmerized by flowing mane
And steady beat of the strike of hooves
Against the stone and ground.
What a wonderful past time I have found.
If you can come ride with me.
Lose track of time upon a horses back.
Don't worry if you feel you can't ride.
I'll teach you…soon you'll get the knack

FARE THEE WELL

Don't mourn for me when I pass on though I'm glad you do
For we had such a good time on this crazy earth
-know that I'll miss you too.
 But did you know my jobs not done?
I still have some work ahead.
I'm going to work in HIS great service
Revelation 19:11-16 haven't you read
Of the armies with white horses and the Faithful and True?
Yes, I'll be there. In white, not brown,
But my shape and nicker will be the same,
So don't mourn with no hope, don't frown.
 But please, my friend, please take note!
In chapter 16, the parable that Doctor Luke wrote,
Head what that Bible of yours has to say;
That Jesus is the Life, the Truth, and the Way.
You must make the choice: To believe is your part.
Get to know Him, my friend,
Love Him and serve Him with all of your heart;
Then your name will be written in the Book.
The angels will rejoice. It is then I can tell
If we ride together again. Fare Thee well. Fare Thee well.

FLEHMEN RESPONSE

Out our camera quickly comes.
Our horse is exposing his teeth and gums.
What a funny way his nose is bent,
For a better analyses of the scent.
Directing "stinky" air up his nose,
Making for a hilarious pose.

HURT

The lead rope clip was lying in my hand
And reaching for the halter of
A pony recently purchased…
My…was he feisty!
Prancing, dancing,
Trying to get to that mare in the field.
I reached for the halter
Before he took off again
Whinnying for his new girl friend.
The clip in my hand,
Ready for action
Was not supposed to cut me.
I never suspected that it would,
But it did.
When the hoof stepped on the dragging rope
The hook from the clip pulled
Catching on the skin
Between my thumb and pointing finger
Ripping a two and a half-inch trail.
I hate to talk of these things,
But to help others not repeat my mistake,
And what precautions to take,
I must.
There was no question that stitches were needed
I didn't have to plead a ride to emergency.
I was quickly taken.
Six shot numbing needles and 25 stitches later
I was on my way.
What a day!

THE RACE

Poised for the start.
Ready to race.
Some jittering and dancing,
Some quietly placed.
A bell for the start
Off goes the pack
Fighting for first
Around the race track.
Goggles in place,
Dirt flung through the air
Being flung up
By hooves without care.
Wind whipping mane,
Stick whipping hide,
Yelling for speed,
A wild fast ride.
Who will be first?
We all do surmise
The horse with most heart
Will win the prize.

WALKING BACK HOME

Our family went to a camp far away
We spent a week training
For the Certified Horsemanship Association.
(Otherwise called the CHA)
There we were introduced to horses-
A big bunch!
We rode them every day after lunch.
We were asked to ride several different mounts
To see how we could handle them.
We went to the trail just plodding along
We felt so good we started singing some songs.
But then we turned around and BAM!
The horse I rode exploded and ran
With his teeth clenched unto his bit
I could not stop…I was sure to hit
The ground with a thud,
But for fear of the thought of landing in mud
I hung on tight.
I tried to steer him with all of my might
Anticipating curves and trees
So he wouldn't smash my knees!
I had never been on such a scary ride,
And I would never forget.
"It may sound fun to you,
Young horse camp riders,
To run back home,
But let's walk, in control," I say
As we ride each summer day.
"I will tell you why, of course,
With a story of my runaway horse."

THE SENTRY

Standing tall,
Alert and aware.
Intensely sniffing, smelling the air.
The whole horse herd is in his care
For danger of mountain lion
Or man, or bear.
Feeling vibrations
Through his hooves in the sand.
When trouble moves
The sentry knows
Whether it is buffalo
Or man.
Ready to fight,
Ready to flee
From any movement he may see.
For the protection of the herd -
His family.
He is the sentry.

DRUGS

That horse didn't get enough of a "cocktail"
What is that supposed to mean?
"They need to be delightful" when what they really are
Remains to be seen.
We had a dose of a drugged up horse
And we learned in a hurry the pain,
To be stuck with a surly, grumpy beast,
And when you thought she was so perfect.
Well…She wasn't perfect in the least!
She pulled on her halter
And bucked people off.
She would rear and twist…
So we put her on our blacklist.
Now what are we supposed to do with a mare
That is dangerous through and through?
Do we drug her again and send her away
For someone else to get hurt on some fateful day?
I would rather take a financial loss
And sell her cheap
To someone that can teach her who is boss,
Than to have someone unknowingly get hurt
Laying bruised and broken in the dirt.
Say no to drugs.
Though they may give someone financial gain,
Sooner or later, drugs will cause pain.

ICE BALLS

They say you get ideas in the act of writing.
I want this poem to be of my growing up years
Of my desires and my fears
Of having horses in the field,
Wanting a barn,
But it was always out of reach, a breach,
Set aside for cows, calves, and pigs.
They stay in their pens and stalls
Dancing their little jigs. Mocking me.
The horses get for their shelter
The side of the hill and trees
When it was cold and blowing,
And snow was falling fast –
Never showing signs of slowing –
I would lie in my warm bed
And pray this weather would not last,
And for God to keep my horses warm,
And see them safely through the storm.
I would think of other places
Where horses didn't have barns or sheds
Hundreds of horses in the snow – just like mine.
If other people do this…
Then my horses should be fine.
But I have to see…So I dress for the cold
And trudge through the field
Sometimes snow is up to my knee.
Looking, looking, like a needle in a haystack
I find them woolly-worm fuzzy.
I find that all I really have to do
Is clean the ice balls from their hooves.

PA'S WORK

Pa worked with heavy harness
Sturdy rugged, rough
As a young boy he learned
How to work
And to be tough
But sometimes to harness each big horse
It took a clever mind
Not brute strength to lift it high
But a pulley Pa did find
Upon the backs the leather laid
A load of weight not born
But just to buckle and to hitch
Then drive the team,
Wagon too,
Out to gather corn.

CARRIAGE HORSE

Beautifully refined,
Shiny with care.
A lofty head tucked into the air.
High stepping dance,
Sturdy and sure,
Strategically displayed,
Eyes to allure.
Carry me along
With your high stepping style.
Carry me along
Oh see the crowd smile.
This dazzling gown,
This smart suited man,
This ornate carriage,
This part of the plan.
The harness of leather laid with silver and gold,
It takes us to the palace I'm told.

Oh sweet dreams…
What fun if they were to come true,
A fine carriage horse? I wish that I knew!
But what I have, I enjoy-this horse friend of mine
As I ride in this little buggy passing some time.
Goldie in harness, brown simple and plain,
Pulling me happily along the quiet lane.
My wonderful buggy horse, you help me to dream
Of your being a carriage horse fit for a queen.

STUCK IN A STALL

I heard of a horse that was stuck in a stall.
Stuck on his back
From rolling, that's all,
But he couldn't get up
With his hooves in the air
He struggled and struggled
With no one to care.
Thankfully someone
Was now passing by
Heard the commotion and came on the fly.
The man tried to pull on the horse's tail
To move him away from the wall. He failed.
The beast was too big.
He ran to get help and some ropes from his rig.
It's a danger to help a horse that is cast
Carefully putting ropes around flailing hooves
Help him roll over - up he comes fast
Much more freedom in the field
This poor fellow will find.
Let him roll and be happy,
And you, the owner,
Will have some peace of mind.

ABUSE

We went to a horse auction
And watched from the sidelines.
Horses and ponies came through the sale ring;
Some skinny from malnutrition,
Some sleek and looking fine.
Then we saw the jerking ropes,
The eyes, scared, white and flitting.
A young boy thinking himself so grand,
With the lead rope a horse head hitting.
"Please stop young man," I loudly said,
"Please have good horsemanship." I pled.
I wondered if he'd understood,
Or if my outburst had done any good.
Then we saw adults with fancy store bought sticks
Whacking on rumps, quivering,
Yearlings huddled in a corner, shivering.
How will the young boy grow? Now I know.

We watch on TV and read in the newspaper,
Situations that cause one to cry.
Horses that look like toothpicks,
And many look ready to die.
Neglected and starving, part of our society is carving
An evil way of existence for horses in their care.
So what do we do when of these situations made aware?
To turn the head and walk away just adds to the despair!
Keep alert, be vigilant. Stop the apathy please!
Go about boldly and courageously
Teaching good horsemanship and responsibility.
It will be a help to horses in situations like these.

FOAL AT DAYBREAK

The misty morning moment
Full of pent up days
Of anticipation and waiting.
"It's here! It's here!"
We are longing to say.
The misty morning moment
Looking through the grass,
And see a patch of color.
With joy our hearts leap.
The foal is here at last!
The foal, small and fragile,
Lays still, very still
We tip toe slowly…A little tail flips
What a thrill!
Up the foal comes on wobbly knees
Looking for mother's milk, its belly to please.
On-lookers come to say "awe" and to stare
At the beautiful foal with the short curly mane.
Waiting for the first soft touch.
Mother horse doesn't seem to complain
But with a soft nicker steps
Between us and the foal.
A good mother, a guard.
She is playing her role.

FEAR

I'm afraid to ride
On this beautiful day.
Fear, oh fear
Please go away!
My heart races and thumps
At the thought of the jumps.
Will my horse rear?
Or runaway?
Will I fall?
Will an ambulance
My friends have to call?
It is sad to say
That maybe in order
For my fears to go away,
I may have to sell
This problem horse.
Or I may have to refresh myself
By going back over
The beginner's course.
I'll do what it takes
To stop the fear.
Maybe now
The answer is clear.
I'll just slow down,
Start over, readjust.
Or I'll build my confidence
In a horse I can trust.

FLIES!

Smack, smack, smack, smack,
We are having a fly attack!
Flies, flies, big and small,
Seems every fly has come to call.

Oh those flies we hate them so.
They cause disruption. They must go!
Bring the sprays, the wipes and rags,
Bug zappers too, and those smelly, fly catching bags.

Remember the days when you just want to have fun…
To enjoy riding your horse under the beautiful sun?
But horses stomp and fuss and shake,
Get rid of the flies for heaven's sake!

But there are some flies that we have found
We don't mind keeping them around.
Fly parasites are small, but they are a mighty force
When you keep them,
You won't have biting flies on your horse.

What parasite flies do
Is eat the bad fly larvae before they can grow
Is there any more information that you need to know?
Oh yes, the cost…Hey, they are well worth the price,
When they keep your horse fly free and acting so nice.

SILVER AND SCOUT

Sometimes the fantasies of my childhood
Could do me lots of good,
For, at times, I dreamed of a different life
Especially, during the long bus ride strife.
The hollering, the jeering, the glaring,
Now out the window staring.
The countryside slips quickly by.
The fantasies started with my hearts cry.
They started with Silver and Scout
Because as a child
I wanted out.
I pretended they ran across western lands
Up trails and down past tumbleweed stands.
Galloping, galloping, working, working,
Their riders, The Lone Ranger and Tanto never shirking
Their responsibility to bring the villain down,
And take them to the jail in town.
I could see those two horses never tiring
Running alongside my bus - men's guns firing.
On through the fields, manes and tails flowing,
Jumping fences, and ditches and creeks, forever going.
This bus ride is over too quickly I shout.
Thanks to you both Silver and Scout.

TACK ROOM

Saddles and bridles lining the wall.
Fourteen, fifteen saddles in all.
Helmets and boots,
Buckles and straps,
A crate full of brushes,
Some well-worn chaps.
A pony harness hanging,
Grain in the big covered can,
Air circulating
With an on-going fan.
This is a place where excitement abounds
Where morning and night
Wranglers are making their rounds.
Many a shoe has come through this door
For the thrill of a ride,
Gaining more knowledge of horses,
Satisfied. They leave.
With anticipation of coming again,
Wanting more.

ALPHA MARE

That's my hay!
That's my stall!
Get out of my way!
I'm boss of all!"

I see the way you command the herd
Your ears laid back, teeth barred for attack.
Away from you, horses run, they race.
You are Alpha Mare. You are first place.
Now you must know, my mare, my mount,
Take this fact into account.
That I'm your Alpha, first place boss,
And with you, I know, I'll suffer no loss.
I choose you
Because of your spirit, your spunk and your flare.
How do I know you and I will be a show winning pair?
Because of you, Alpha, first place mare.

SNICKERS

Pony, you make me laugh.
Your antics entertain.
When in the pasture
We played a baseball game.
Down the nipped down field,
The ball was hit,
It was you, pony, who ran after it.
You beat us to that ball and bit,
And ran away with that ball,
Your lips turned up
Prancing, dancing.
While you were having so much fun…
Your antics gave the other team
The home run.

MUD

The nastiest sight I ever did see
Was the time mud came
To torment me.
Up past my ankles
sloshing around.
Making the trek to the feeder
A memorable ground.
My boot got stuck, and I toppled down
With a mud sucking sound and a squeal
To the soft squishy ground.
Eeeeww and ick.
My clothes look sick.
Hey! Did I just hear a camera click?
Go on and take pictures, go on, I guess.
Someone's got to get some
Humor out of this mess.

SWEET, SWEET SOUND

When we go to the barn
We hear a sweet, sweet sound
Of nickers and whinnies
And hooves pounding the ground.
Here they come
On the run.
We know we're going to
Have some fun.
Do they like the brushing?
Do they like the treat?
Do they like the flake of hay
We throw down at their feet?
Do they like the time we ride them?
Up and down the trails?
They must because we don't see
Swishing, angry tails.
We treat them well
We treat them right
We know why they run to us
When we are in their sight.
To them,
We are the sweet, sweet sound.

RED MARK'S LEGACY

The huge Tennessee Walker,
Full of precision and energy,
Came to our barn one day.
She hadn't been around her own kind
For a long, long time.
Her antics included
A nose touch; then a dreaded pee spray.
What a terrible thing to do!
For weeks it continued on…
(Well…it continued for days)
And in my mind I conjured up ways
To politely send her back -still.
Deep in my heart
There was a word of debate.
Wait.
Take some time
And let her settle down.
Then a gelding friend she found.
She stayed by him
All of the time
She acted like taking him
For a ride was a crime.
She paced
Up and down the fence
Nickering.
She changed.
Now, what a glorious mare she is.
Her presence is an eye catcher.
Her attitude has mellowed.
I am glad she is here.

MANURE PILE

It never fails to accumulate.
This happens to be
A horse lover's fate.
Of course of you happen to be
Rich enough to hire a person like me,
You will not have to do this necessity.
But you better be nice to the people you hire,
Or you will be
Forever returning to your horses mire?
Be nice and generous to your help…
Give them some smiles,
With words of kindness for shoveling the piles.

TWINKIE BANDITS

Those childhood days of pony fun
Riding to the neighbor's house at a pony run.
Playing cowboys and Indians,
And cops and robbers and tag,
On the way to the corner store
For some treats in a bag.
In the store parking lot, just off the street
The Twinkie delivery man we did meet.
Up went our handkerchief masks
Our fingers became a gun
In our western voice we said
"Hey there, good buddy,
Ya bedder hand over some."
We were just playing
Did he hear the giggle in our voice?
We were only 9 and 10
To give or not? He had a choice.
To our surprise
He gave us each one
Our masks came off
Gone was our finger gun
"Thank you mister
You are awful kind
A better Twinkie delivery man
We cannot find."

MERRY-GO-ROUND

Graceful horses in a row
In their finery, posing,
Ready to go.
Hard and smooth,
Glossed to a sheen
I choose my mount
With eye agleam.
My 4-H friends choose too,
And we have fun.
Pretending to race
The music's begun
Around, around,
Around we go.
Spectators watch.
Our antics grow.

They say,
"Is this the 4-H group
That we know?"
In our matching
Shirts and jeans
And hats and ties,
We are a sight
For laughing eyes.
With our hey-ya's and hoots
And our shouts to gad-de-up,
We pretend to ride jockey style
Racing in the Breeder's cup.

PRESENT FROM MY PA

The present from my pa
Was the life that he loved
Filled with horses.
From the big work horses,
Fanny and Don,
To the prancing ponies
Forever filling our lives
Seeing their silly antics.
Stories came from them,
And we would laugh and learn.
We always had something
To talk about,
For the horse was a common ground.
It was time well spent…
Talking about the horses
Led to talking about other things in life.
It was a present from my Pa.

FANNY AND DON

Pa, you had Fanny and Don, a working horse pair;
That when talking of them made everyone aware
How decked out in harness with the tugs in place,
The team was ready to pull.
I can just see the smile on your face.
You taught your horses so well.
You had to be so proud-Showing off your horse;s talents.
I just wish there could have a crowd.
But you did your long hours of work
In the quiet rolling fields.
On the farm that was your home, you brought in the yields.
You talk of those days with a smile and a sigh.
Fanny and Don were your friends and pals.
Did you spend the time talking to them?
And in problems confide?
Now as you feebly sit in your chair,
You talk of their care -The big Belgium pair.
To me a story of the past.
To you a precious memory that would last.

DEATH - THE FALL IN 1990

Death is inevitable. Death will happen.
It happened to my horse.
It was an odd time of the year
For him to be born
So late in the year on Veterans Day.
I had good dreams for this horse.
He ran with his dam in the big field
Away from Barns and houses
On a lonely stretch of road
We came and went regularly
Taking care that all the horses were well,
And a year passed swiftly by. Veteran grew.
I had dreams for this horse
He would be big and flashy
Like his sire. Big and beautiful
It was my desire
To have big dreams this horse
But it all ended with a shot.
Where these horses had run
Season after season, year after year
People knew they were there.
But of poachers beware!
They came by night with a strong deer-shining light
Those poachers – encroachers!
Saw Veterans eyes…shining eyes…and fired.
He was the size of a large deer at a year
The gun was fired. Veteran lay dead.
And so lay my big dreams with him.

SCARS

Scars tell a story
In Belephantaine
About a horse
Who had a huge scar
That stretched far
Across his rump.
It was crooked and gruesome-
A senseless thing,
Like a sports car with a huge ding.
When asked,
"How did your horse get that thing?"
It was answered, "Don't know,
But people had worked hard
To find out and scoured the area
Where the horse was pastured,
But nothing was found to show
What caused the eyesore."
Couldn't they have looked some more?
Perhaps a jagged broke off branch,
A piece of half buried glass,
A spike in a fence post?
An old rusty latch?
"An ounce of prevention
Is worth a pound of cure."
Do not stop looking
Until you're absolutely sure.
It would be very sad of course,
If the same kind of scar
Showed up on another horse.

FEED STORE IMAGINATIONS

There's a little electrical bike at the feed store.
We saw it today as we asked
The price of grain and hay.
It was small with yellow fenders.
I'm surprised they let me ride it,
Lickety split,
Up and down the isles.
Better slow down, I thought
Don't want to crash.
These mountain people are
So laid back.
They don't act at all
Like they are going
To have a heart attack.
I'm thinkin' 'bout buyin' that little bike.
Scootin' along to the horse pasture
Would be so fine,
But better have an orange flag
Cause of all the traffic goin' by.
...and those large trucks full of coal
...And the many blind curves
...And no shoulders to the road
"I don't want to die!" I shout.
…let's see
…I don't want that bike after all
So the next time we go to the feed store
We just buy the grain
And get out.

BARBED WIRE

Every mention or thought of barbed wire
Brings bad memories and raises my ire.
In the past I have worked with it.
I have helped string it out.
It usually brought more than one shout.
Stop! Help! Ouch! Wait!
Frustrated. Furious! Barbed Wire I Hate!
Many animals on Pa's farm
Were cut…some severe.
I would say get that wicked stuff out if here!
…It didn't go off the farm
But stayed year after rusting year

Now it has pretty much gone
For time has taken its toll.
As time permits
Through the old farm land I stroll
Remembering where once large herds
The fields would boast
Now I see bits and pieces
Of rusted wire here and there
Dangling from rotted, tipping fence posts.
Should my family ever again farm,
Should it be nephew, grandson or any of my kin,
I would raise my old feeble voice
And sound an alarm.
No more barbed wire!
Keep your animals from undue harm.

THE NIPPER SOLUTION

Hug a horse's head
And you will see
A change
In his personality.
Pet him,
Stroke him,
Rub his nose.
Push him away
When he nibbles
On your clothes.
With your fingers
His forelock comb.
Rub him under is head
Between his jawbone.
Don't just stand there
And wait for him to bite,
And don't expect change
To happen overnight.
Stop him, back him up, go forward, turn.
Eventually he will learn.
He'll be so busy doing what you ask
That thinking about biting
Will be a fading task.

THE SMELL OF LEATHER

There is something about
The smell of leather
As I walk through a mall
And pass by the store.
That intoxicating smell
Of leather draws me in.
(Not that I will buy something.
Usually my pocketbook
Cannot afford it.)
To just look and breathe deep.
To touch the soft suppleness
Of coat and purse,
(Surely this isn't a curse!)
The lasting smoothness
Of wallet and hat
The smell pulls me to want
Something like that.

There is something about
The sight of a horse under saddle.
That saddle and bridle and breast collar
All matching, all studded with silver
And clean and polished.
Seeing that horse hard at work
Under that array,
Like a 5th avenue, suited, brief-cased business man,
Doing his work
With top notch precision and finesse,
Pulls me to want something like that.

CHRISTMAS TRIP

Early in the morning
Before the sun rises
We wake up and prepare
To head to the North land.
Everything is packed
Into the white truck and trailer.
Carrying suitcases,
And Christmas presents,
And so forth.
All packed? Ready to Go?
Of course!
Then we drive to pick up Abbey
The big, black Christmas horse.
She is a present for a 13 year old girl.
It really worked out well
For we considered this horse to sell.
Abbey was older in age
And the rigors of the camp horse
Were not for her.
The lady we were giving her to
Worked out a trade, two for one.
We were getting the small Hefflingers
Who were not comfortable to ride.
She was getting a sweet gentle mare-
Two great needs collide.
So while we visit family and friends
And enjoy the beautiful snow,
Three horses find a new place in life
New kids they will get to know.

MAGNIFICENT OBSESSION

What is it in the people who have ridden so long?
Who may have been hurt by the beast?
Still again they try to mount up and ride
And they aren't fearful in the least.
What is it in those people?
What is it that makes them tick?
What an obsession they have!
To horses and riding they surely stick.
Would Christopher Reeves have rode again?
Had he recovered?
We would have to say, YES!
A magnificent obsession he had discovered.
If only there were some sort of salve
One could rub on to make one have
Such an obsession with life and living.
Priceless salve well worth getting and giving
As like the obsession the true horseman has with his horse.
It is a magnificent obsession.

BOOT SCRAMBLE

Little boots in a pile.
Little boots every color and style.
Mostly browns and shiny blacks
Cowboy boots in piles and stacks.

It was a pony race to see
Who could find their boots and be
Racing fast, racing fine,
The first to cross the finish line.

On your marks! Get set! Go!
Ponies running fast and slow.
Stop! Dismount fast and slick
Find your boots now. Quick! Quick! Quick!

Now how am I supposed to see?
Which brown boots belong to me?
Boots thrown here, boots thrown there.
Racing, running, find my pair.

Mount my pony, turn and run.
Galloping ponies, oh, what fun.
When the pony race was through,
The winner's boots were bright sky blue!

PALM SUNDAY

I have raised horses,
Babes who have run in the pasture,
Running free,
Until they met me.
And things changed.
It wasn't easy.
It took lots of time
To accomplish the task
Of acceptance and compliance.
Of obedience.
It took lots of time -
Days and months of time.
So…
I am amazed
How a donkey
Who had never been ridden
Could accept a man,
And accept palm branches,
And coats, and noises of hundreds
Being thrown before him.
This could not have happened
For me...or you,
But for Jesus
The donkey went.

HORSE SHOW DAYS

Oh those wonderful
Horse Show days of the past,
When thinking of memory after memory,
I wished those days
Would come again and cast
A childhood life upon me once more.
The things we did…to tell it seems like folklore.
As young pre-teens
We rode our ponies eight miles into town
(I'm sure nowadays that would bring a frown)
Riding down the lonely dirt rode
Taking the back way
Past pastures of interested horses or cows,
And waving at farmers making hay.
Feeling important and special
Crossing mainstreet,
Hearing the pony's clippity, clopping
With their dainty little feet,
And knowing attention
Would come our way…(We were just 12)
Oh, if we could do this every day.
Going to the fairgrounds
Where they hold the horse shows
And on to the horse barn
And meeting our families
With our camping stuff.
Our excitement grows.
We're going to spend the night here, and sleep
In the sawdust horse barn isle on bales of hay.
Mom and dad's stay long enough to say
"You be careful and good."
With a big grin we say "OK,"
And older brothers
Camp nearby for our protection at night.
Mom and Dad feel
That everything will be alright
…..And we grin.
Oh the things we did that night.

HORSE SHOW DAYS (continued)

Riding our ponies around the race track
In the pale moonlight.
Walking through
The empty Grand Stand rows
Dreaming of tomorrow
When it would be filled
With people watching the horse show.
Back at the barn
Our ponies nicker our return
Cleaning and brushing and thinking to earn
A big colorful ribbon
And be applauded our due.
Then we heard our brothers yell,
"Go to bed you two!"
"We must brush our teeth
And clean up a bit."
So we darted across
The road in the dark to the airport lobby
And said to each other,
"What good luck we've hit!"
For no one was there.
It was cozy and clean.
We shoved our hands into our pockets
For coins
To drop into the hot chocolate machine.
We went to the bathroom
Where no night watchman would bother
Stuck our feet in the sink
And turned on the hot water.
And we sipped our hot chocolate and giggled awhile
As we drew faces in the steamed up mirror.
(That memory makes me smile)
The next day
We were up early and ready to go
As horse trailer after horse trailer arrived for the show.
We looked at each other with a twinkle in our eye.
The night has been fun.
Now let's give this day a try.

www.ingramcontent.com/pod-product-compliance
Lightning Source LLC
Chambersburg PA
CBHW060545030426
42337CB00021B/4440